FROM SLAVE BOY TO BISHOP

Samuel Adjai Crowther (1809–1892) led an
exciting and adventurous life. Born in a west
African village, he was captured and sold as a
slave. After a dramatic rescue he became a
Christian. He travelled extensively, founding
many Christian missions. He translated the Bible
into Yoruba, and became the first black Anglican
bishop.

STORIES OF FAITH AND FAME

BISHOP JIM
Joyce Reason — The story of James Hannington

CONQUEROR OF DARKNESS
Phyllis Garlick — The story of Helen Keller

CRUSADER FOR CHRIST
Jean Wilson — The story of Billy Graham

EVER OPEN DOOR
C. Scott — The story of Dr Barnado

FRIEND OF THE CHIEFS
Iris Clinton — The story of Robert Moffat

FROM SLAVE BOY TO BISHOP
John Milsome — The story of Samuel Adjai Crowther

GOD'S ARCTIC ADVENTURER
Constance Savery — The story of William Bompas

GOD'S MADCAP
Nancy E. Robbins — The story of Amy Carmichael

GOLDEN FOOT
J. R. Batten — The story of Judson of Burma

HORSEMAN OF THE KING
Cyril Davey — The story of John Wesley

NIGHT OF THE SNOWS
R. G. Martin — The story of Wilfred Grenfell

LADY WITH A LAMP
Cyril Davey — The story of Florence Nightingale

MILLIONAIRE FOR GOD
J. Erskine — The story of C. T. Studd

NEVER SAY DIE
Cyril Davey — The story of Gladys Aylward

ON THE CLOUDS TO CHINA
Cyril Davey — The story of Hudson Taylor

PROPHET OF THE PACIFIC
Margaret Kabell — The story of John G. Paton

QUAKER CAVALIER
Joyce Reason — The story of William Penn

SEARCHER FOR GOD
Joyce Reason — The story of Isobel Kuhn

SLAVE SHIP CAPTAIN
Carolyn Scott — The story of John Newton

SOUTH SEAS SAILOR
Cecil Northcott — The story of John Williams

STAR OVER GOBI
Cecil Northcott — The story of Mildred Cable

THE DOCTOR WHO NEVER GAVE UP
C. Scott — The story of Dr Ida Scudder

THE HEROINE OF NEWGATE
John Milsome — The story of Elizabeth Fry

THE MAN WHO FREED THE SLAVES
Elsie M. Johnson — The story of William Wilberforce

THE MONK WHO SHOOK THE WORLD
Cyril Davey — The story of Martin Luther

TO BE A PILGRIM
Joyce Reason — The story of John Bunyan

TRAIL MAKER
R. V. Latham — The story of David Livingstone

WHITE QUEEN
Donald McFarlan — The story of Mary Slessor

WIZARD OF THE GREAT LAKE
Donald McFarlan — The story of Alexander Mackay

YOUNG MAN IN A HURRY
Iris Clinton — The story of William Carey

FROM SLAVE BOY TO BISHOP

The Story of Samuel Adjai Crowther

by
JOHN MILSOME

LUTTERWORTH PRESS
Cambridge

For Odette and David

Lutterworth Press
7 All Saints' Passage
Cambridge CB2 3LS

British Library Cataloguing in Publication Data

Milsome, John
From slave boy to bishop: the story of Samuel
Adjai Crowther.—(Stories of faith and fame).
1. Crowther, Samuel—Juvenile literature
2. Church of England—Bishops—Biography—
Juvenile literature 3. Missionaries—Nigeria
—Biography—Juvenile literature 4. Bishops
—Nigeria—Biography—Juvenile literature
I. Title   II. Series
283′.092′4   BV3625.N6C7

ISBN 0-7188-2678-7

Cover illustrations and maps by Elissa Vial
Copyright © Lutterworth Press 1987
First published 1987 by Lutterworth Press

Typeset in Monophoto Plantin Medium by
Vision Typesetting, Manchester

Made and printed in Great Britain by
The Guernsey Press Co. Ltd., Guernsey, Channel Islands.

CONTENTS

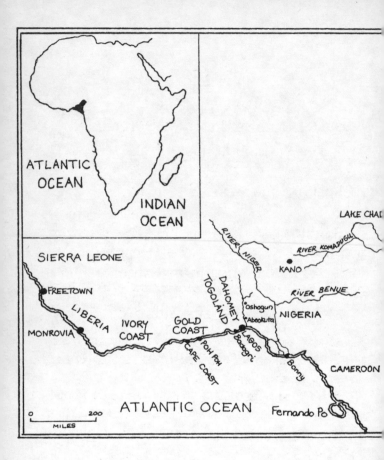

ATLANTIC
OCEAN

INDIAN
OCEAN

LAKE CHAD

RIVER NIGER

RIVER KOMADUGU

KANO

RIVER BENUE

SIERRA LEONE

Freetown

LIBERIA

IVORY
COAST

GOLD
COAST

DAHOMEY
TOGOLAND

Oshogun
Abeokuta

NIGERIA

MONROVIA

CAPE COAST

Poh Poh

LAGOS
Badagri

Bonny

CAMEROON

ATLANTIC OCEAN

Fernando Po

0   200
MILES

1

EARLY YEARS IN OSHOGUN

"WE have consulted the oracle," said the Ifa priest. "And we have a name for the baby."

This was the moment the crowd had been waiting for and they listened quietly. The baby was a boy, eight days old, when according to Yoruba tradition in that part of West Africa, he had to be named. The Yoruba family and their friends had watched while the priest held a carved wooden Ifa Bowl and shuffled thirty split palm nuts in it. He had counted the whites from the browns and from this he could interpret the decision of the Yoruba gods.

"We asked which of the 401 Yoruba gods our child was to worship and we have been told that he is a child of Olorun. Therefore he should worship Olorun, the one supreme god."

There was some murmuring among the members of the family as such an announcement was unusual but the priest silenced them and went on speaking. "This child is to be named Adjai: a name that means that he is destined for a remarkable future."

It was hot under that African sun as the crowd moved away from the shade of the trees and made their way towards one of the gates of Oshogun. In

1809 Oshogun was a large town for that part of West Africa. It was situated by the River Ogun and had a population of about twelve thousand people. As it was a time of war, strangers were unwelcome and a high wooden fence surrounded the town. There were six gates into Oshogun and these were always kept guarded.

Adjai's father and his mother, Afala, had hoped for a more ordinary name for their son. They had already given gifts of white fowls. Now they paid their fee to the priest in cowrie shells before returning to their home in Oshogun. As Adjai's father was a member of an important Yoruba family they lived in one of the biggest houses in the compound, built of decorated red clay and with a roof of clay and wood thatch. Adjai's parents were wealthy people, his father following the family tradition of weaving special quality cloth. He was also a headman with some authority in the town.

Celebrations followed the naming ceremony, and Adjai's parents accepted the gifts and good wishes of their friends and relatives. Then baby Adjai was taken into the house again with his parents, grandparents, brothers and sisters and everything returned to normal. The people of Oshogun could not spend too much time in celebrations. They had to be always on their guard against possible attack; for this was not a happy time in that part of West Africa, where there was often fighting between the inhabitants of different towns.

Around the house of Adjai's family was a wall

of reeds. There was an opening in the wall which led into the family compound where there were several small huts used for storing food, clothing and weapons. If the town was to be attacked, the farmers could grab the bows, arrows and spears in the storage huts and become fighting warriors.

Adjai did not have many years to play with his brothers, sisters and friends. While he was very young he would sometimes make toys from soft clay and then leave them to harden in the burning sun. He became very good at modelling clay animals and toy pots. As he grew older he would jump on one of the goats that wandered about in the compound and ride it, pretending he was on a horse.

When he was about eight years of age, Adjai had to work with his big brother Bola, helping him do all kinds of jobs in the compound, running errands and sometimes going to their father's farm. In time Adjai kept chickens of his own, breeding and reselling them. He had a small piece of land in a corner of the farm where he grew crops of yams, pleasant tasting sweet potatoes. He did a good trade with his yams and chickens, once filling a long piece of string with cowrie shell money.

The boys of Adjai's age were put into groups of about forty and sent to work on one of the farms. Adjai was made a leader of a group. He thought nothing of getting up very early in the morning and walking more than 12 kilometres while the air was still cool until he reached the farm. There he would gather his crop of yams and then wait for the other boys to arrive. While they were busy in the hot sun hoeing the earth, Adjai would be watching them from the shade of the nearest tree.

It was the Yoruba custom to keep carvings of gods in their houses and Adjai's father was no exception. One day he was standing in the compound talking to his brother Bola when their two sisters came running from the house shouting for help.

"What's the matter?" Adjai asked, trying to calm his sister.

"There's been an accident," gasped one girl, hardly able to get her breath. "The house is on fire."

Sure enough Bola and Adjai could see smoke rising from the roof. Then their mother appeared at the door. She was coughing and could not speak for some moments.

"It's all right," she managed to say at last. "There's nobody in there, but the gods will burn."

Adjai knew how important these Yoruba gods were to his father and his family. He ran to the door but at first was driven back by the smoke and flames. Then he remembered his father saying how once he had escaped from a forest fire by crouching down as low as he could. So Adjai crawled along the floor of the house until he reached the place where he thought the gods were displayed. At first with all the smoke around him he couldn't see properly but suddenly he could feel one of the carvings. Then another one. He picked them up and crawled back to the door. He did this again and again until all the carved gods were saved.

By then many members of his family, friends and others were in the compound. When Adjai appeared with all the carvings, they clapped and cheered him. It was a very proud moment for the young African boy. The house had been destroyed by the fire and had to be rebuilt but all the Yoruba gods belonging to the family had been rescued thanks to Adjai.

One day when Adjai and Bola did not have to work on the farm they went to their mother and asked if they could go to the River Ogun for a while to catch fish. She was already busy helping other friends and relatives to weave and embroider beautiful fabrics to be sold in the local market. There was still some work to be done on the roof thatching of the new house and the red earth of the walls was not finished.

"There's plenty of work to do here," said Afala. "You can go for a short time but make sure you bring me back some fish."

"We promise we will," shouted the boys as they ran off with their nets before their mother could change her mind.

They soon found a good place to fish where there were lots of trees and long grass by the river bank. The boys knew there were snakes and crocodiles about and so they had to keep on the alert. Although they hung their net in the water for some time they only caught two very small fish. Bola threw them back into the water.

"It's not worth taking them home," he said.

"We'll have to catch some," said Adjai. "Otherwise our mother will never believe we've been fishing."

Suddenly their friend Okanbi came into view in his small boat. He waved and paddled across to them. When he came close they could see that he had made a good catch of fish.

"When you stand in the water with your net, the fish can see you and you frighten them away," laughed Okanbi, noticing their nets were empty.

"Can we come with you?" Bola asked. "Perhaps then we'll be lucky."

"My canoe is too small," said Okanbi. "Instead of catching fish, you would be eaten by a crocodile."

While Adjai and Bola argued with Okanbi they caught one more very small fish. Okanbi felt so sorry for them that he let them sit in his canoe with their net in the water. They passed several crocodiles and the boys began to feel nervous. Then suddenly they could see lots of fish swimming round them. When they lifted the net from the water, it was bulging. After the rainy season the river was very wide and the bank looked a long way off.

"I think we should return home now," said Okanbi and his friends agreed. As they looked across at the river bank, the grass began to sway and the trees were rustled by a sudden wind. It had been sunny and hot but there was a slight wind and the approaching clouds gave a hint of rain. The river would not be a good place to be if the rain should start. So Okanbi turned his boat towards the bank and paddled as fast as he could, with Adjai and Bola trying to help by paddling with their hands.

"Careful!" Shouted Okanbi as the boat wobbled and tilted dangerously. "You'd better leave it to me."

As soon as they reached the bank they hurried back to Oshogun. The sky had changed from bright sunshine to grey clouds.

The boys knew that before the dry season started there could be a few more violent rainstorms. They had just reached one of the gates of the town when the rain came down in a torrential storm, soaking them and washing away some of their catch. Fortunately the boys still had some fish in their nets to show their mother.

"You have done well," she said. "I'll cook those fish for all of us tonight."

The boys were glad it was raining as they would not now have to work outside in the compound. Their sister was making a design on a calabash with a charred stick from the fire. When she saw them idly watching her, she protested that there were more calabashes to be made.

"You can help your sister," said their mother and although they grumbled the boys set to work.

There were many gourd plants growing in the compound and this latest rainstorm would be good for them. The gourd shells dried and became very hard. Then they could be made into calabashes and used as jugs and bowls. Adjai's sister was especially skilful at doing beautifully designed patterns on the calabashes which decorated their home.

Both Bola and Adjai had bows and arrows of their own and knew how to use them for hunting. If ever enemies threatened Oshogun the boys could use their skills with the bow to fight them. Their chance came in 1821 when Adjai was twelve years of age. His father had gone with Bola to work on his farm but at first Adjai stayed at home. Then his mother remembered that she needed some yams and asked Adjai to go to the farm to get them.

Adjai usually carried his bow and quiver of arrows when he left home. There might be a chance to use them for hunting on the way and although he didn't anticipate any danger, it gave him a feeling of safety to be carrying his bow and arrows. Thousands of the men of the town had gone off early that morning to their farms for there was much work to be done. Adjai looked at the bowl his mother had given him. It was large and would hold a lot of yams. The walk back from the farm would be long, hot and very tiring.

So Adjai lingered over his breakfast that morning. Then when his mother reminded him about the yams, he said goodbye to her, his grandmother and sisters and set off for the town gate. He walked slowly, thinking that if he was lucky, he might get a lift from a farmer riding on horseback.

Oshogun seemed a quiet place that morning.

14

There were so many away on their farms. Many of the women and children were busy in their homes.

"Where are you going Adjai?" Called Ojo, one of Adjai's friends.

"I'm going to the farm to get some yams," said Adjai. "Do you want to come with me?"

Ojo had come out of his compound to escape having to do work there. "Yes, I would like to come," he said.

The two boys walked to the gate. There they stood in the shade of the town fence and looked along the dusty road into the distance. Suddenly Ojo pointed.

"What's that thing coming towards us?" He said.

When Adjai looked, he could see a big cloud of dust that seemed to be moving. Then he realised what they were.

"It's horsemen, but why are they galloping so fast?"

The gateman was looking worried. He shouted warnings and quickly some men appeared by the gate, armed with spears and bows and arrows. The approaching horsemen were waving and shouting.

"You boys, go back home," called the gateman.

Adjai and his friend turned to go but suddenly Adjai stopped. He recognised one of the horsemen who had reached the gate. It was his father, shouting a warning that an enemy army was not

15

far away and was coming to attack Oshogun. Adjai ran to his father who was bleeding from a wound on his face.

"Don't worry," said his father. "It's nothing."

Then he lifted his son onto the horse and rode to their house. Here Adjai heard him explaining how he had been attacked by a mixed force of the Foulah Tribe, Yoruba Moslems and ex-slaves who had joined them in hope of plunder. With the help of the other farmers, Adjai's father had managed to make his escape back to Oshogun.

There was no time for further explanations. Adjai's father took weapons from the store and went to join the other men of Oshogun who were fighting to defend their town. It was the last time Adjai and the rest of the family saw their father alive. The women and children ran to their homes but Adjai hesitated. He still had his bow and five arrows. Perhaps he could do something to help.

Near the high fence that went all round Oshogun was a tree that Adjai had often climbed in the past to watch merchants and others as they rode towards the town. He again climbed the tree but this time he saw a large army approaching Oshogun at a terrifying speed. They attacked the town on all sides.

The men of Oshogun fought back with great bravery trying to prevent the enemy smashing a way through the fence and gates. There was no relief for the defenders however. As soon as one crowd of the attackers was forced back, another huge force launched a new attack. For a time the

Foulah and their allies could not gain entry into the town.

Another violent attack and parts of the fence crashed down bringing a crowd of Oshogun men to try to hold the enemy back while repairs were done. It was too late and in spite of valiant efforts by the townspeople, they were outnumbered, and shouting their war cries, the Foulah entered Oshogun. From his vantage point in the tree, Adjai could see what was happening. He tried to shoot an arrow at the enemy but it fell well short of its target. The fence came down and the invaders came rushing through the gap.

This time they did not get far before they were cut down by the desperate defenders. Another attack caused some of the Oshogun men to leave the gate they were defending to help others who were trying to repair the fence. By weight of numbers the Foulah began to force their way into the town. There were buildings in flames with the fires spreading rapidly on all sides. The Foulah were advancing until there were thousands in the burning town and the men of Oshogun were on the retreat.

Women, who had quickly thrown their possessions into baskets and were carrying their babies on their backs, tried to run away and escape to the open countryside. Many injured themselves on the prickly bushes that were everywhere. Adjai could hear their screams of pain and fear as they were caught, tied up and dragged away by the Foulah warriors.

He recognised many of his friends and relatives in this line of prisoners. Then to his horror he saw his mother, his brother Joseph and his sister had been captured. His grandmother was a very determined old lady but now she had a rope round her neck and could do nothing to resist. At the sight of his grandmother being dragged roughly into the line of prisoners, Adjai climbed down from the tree.

"Let her alone!" he shouted.

He did not shout for long. A rope was flung round him and pulled tight, so that he could hardly move his arms. Then he too was pushed into what was now a long column of Oshogun prisoners.

"Start moving," called a Foulah soldier, bringing a thick stick down on the shoulders of the man at the front. The man stumbled forward, followed by a long line of frightened prisoners. As they walked through the forest, past other burnt out villages, the rumour spread from one prisoner to another that they were going to Neh'i to be sold into slavery.

2

SOLD INTO SLAVERY

"LET us be sold as a family," said Adjai's mother.

They were in Neh'i, the main town for slave trading in that region. All the people from Oshogun had been assembled, tired and fearful of what was going to happen to them. In the slave market, local chieftains could purchase the people that they thought would make suitable slaves. Adjai's family had managed to keep together for a time but now he and his sister were being examined by a chieftain.

"These will do," said the chieftain. "I will take them now."

"Are they going to Dahdah?" Shouted Adjai's mother who had just been sold to a man living in that town.

The slave trader shook his head. The chief had paid a good price for the boy and girl, so they would have to go with him. There was some argument between the trader and the chief who was having second thoughts about having Adjai's sister. In the end he decided not to buy her and instead she was purchased by the man from Dahdah and reunited with her mother.

By a strange stroke of fate the chieftain who had bought Adjai found that his horse was lame.

19

He wanted to leave straight away for his own village but was unsure whether his horse would manage the journey, so he exchanged Adjai for a new horse. This animal proved to be in even worse condition than his own horse, but Adjai was once again back with a merchant going to Dahdah.

There was great excitement when he reached that town and saw his family and friends again. Adjai, who was twelve years old, found himself working for a man who owned many horses. Often in the past he had helped his father look after horses and he was skilled at this work. His master was well pleased with him and Adjai was employed both looking after horses and working on a nearby farm.

Sometimes there was talk of people being taken to the coast to be sold as slaves and sent across the sea to strange lands. This happened especially to people who were taken first to the slave markets in the Poh Poh country. Weeks went by however and with his mother and sister still in Dahdah, Adjai began to feel quite settled and happy. Perhaps after all, nothing very terrible would happen to them and one day they could go back to Oshogun and rebuild the town.

He would often talk to his friend Oko who had also come from Oshogun. The two boys worked together on the farm and Oko always grumbled to Adjai about the way he was treated.

"It's best to keep such thoughts to yourself," said Adjai. "If the master hears of the things you

20

say about him, I think he'll make you work even harder."

Oko was always bringing bad news about other boys from Oshogun. He especially noticed when someone was missing and guessed at the fate that had befallen them. Adjai was only too aware that many of his old friends had gone.

"I am sure they have been sent to Poh Poh country," said Oko one day when another boy slave they had known in Oshogun suddenly disappeared. Adjai was still happy in Dahdah and hoped he would never have to leave. Then the next day he had a shock for Oko had gone.

"Where is my friend Oko?" He asked one of the men who worked on the farm but lived in Dahdah.

"He was lazy and always grumbling and so the master has sent him to Ijahi."

Adjai asked no more questions. He had heard talk of the big slave market in Ijahi. Sometimes traders came from the Poh Poh country to buy slaves at this market and then resell them at a big profit on the West African coast. Poor Oko! Adjai hoped that this would not be his friend's fate.

More weeks went by and Adjai continued to hope that he would not be sent away. He worked hard and his master never complained about him. Perhaps he would be able to stay in Dahdah until the day he and his family were set free. Then the morning came when he was told that he would not be going to the farm again. Some men came and told him to get ready to join a group of

21

people who were leaving Dahdah.

"Why do I have to go?" asked Adjai.

"Don't ask questions. Just come with us," replied one of the men, taking hold of Adjai's arm in a firm grip as Adjai struggled to get free.

"Let me see my mother and sister before I go," he shouted.

The man became angry and called to some other slave traders. They were carrying chains which they soon fixed to Adjai's ankles and wrists, so that he had no hope of escape. He was forced to join a group, some chained like himself, and made to walk through the forest. Although Adjai was terrified at the thought of being sold as a slave, it was a relief to reach Ijahi and be released from the chains.

Here he had to stand with others in the slave market. People came to look at him to see if he might make a good worker for them. They asked the trader where the boy came from and what work he had done before. The trader, hoping to make a good profit, naturally praised Adjai as a good hard-working boy.

At last a woman from the village of Toko became interested. She had a boy with her of about the same age as Adjai. He smiled and seemed friendly. There was some haggling over the price before the woman bought Adjai and took him to Toko.

For some months Adjai was a slave boy in this village. Life was not too unpleasant for him. Although he was a slave and missed his family he was well treated by his new mistress. Her son was friendly and often talked and played with Adjai, so he was not lonely.

Much of the time he was free to walk about the village but he knew that if he tried to escape he would not get far before he was sure to be caught. In any case it was possible that by now his mother, sister and others in his family might have left Dahdah. He had not seen his brother Joseph for a long time and had no idea where he might be by now.

The dreaded day came when he heard people talking about the Poh Poh country. Slave traders were coming to Toko to buy slaves to be taken to this terrible place where the slaves were put in a market near the sea. Here strange men came to take the slaves away in their ships for ever. There were tales of misery on these ships where people died at sea. Those that survived faced a life of slavery far from home.

When Adjai heard his mistress talking about the Poh Poh country with her son, he knew that his days in the village were coming to an end. Once again he thought of trying to escape but if he was caught, he would be even more cruelly treated, beaten and then chained for his journey to the coast. So when the slave traders from Poh Poh came, Adjai said goodbye to his mistress and her son and accepted his fate.

The trek to I'ko-sy was through hot, wet tropical forest. Travelling was a misery with some of the slaves dropping with exhaustion, only to be whipped until they staggered to their feet and somehow managed to keep moving.

Others became ill with fever and were left to die.

Adjai survived the journey, showing the strength and stamina that was to be typical of him in later life. When at last he was put to stand with the slaves in the market he was surprised and overjoyed to hear a familiar voice calling him. He looked round to see his brother.

"Joseph! You are still safe," shouted Adjai as he embraced his brother.

The two brothers had had similar experiences after surviving the battle for Oshogun in 1821. They had both worked for different slave owners only to end at the same slave market in I'ko-sy. At first no one bought the boys. They saw others depart on the big sailing boats but Adjai and Joseph remained in the coastal market. They had never before seen such huge boats with great billowing sails, manned by strange looking seamen who came from lands far away and could not speak the Yoruba language.

Then a new ship anchored off the shore. It was a Portuguese vessel named the *Esperanza Felix*. The captain came ashore to the slave market to buy his quota of slaves. When he had finished his inspection of the market, 187 people stood in a separate group to be made ready to board the slave ship. Included in their number were Adjai and Joseph.

With the other slaves, the boys were crowded into the hold of the ship. They could hardly breathe. It was extremely hot and there was not enough air. The captain had chosen people in the market who looked young and fit for many years of work. Even so, he knew that many of them might die during the voyage to South America because of the dreadful conditions on the ship.

Naturally the slaves wondered about their destination. One had heard talk about an island called Sao Tome where these slave ships sometimes went. He had heard that this island was not too far from Africa and it was even possible for a slave there to think of getting back to his homeland. Another man said he had heard from a seaman that from Sao Tome they could be sent to a far away country across the ocean, called Brazil. Such gossip meant little to Adjai. He could see no hope of ever seeing Africa again and even less hope of being reunited with his family.

3

RESCUED

AS it happened the slaves on the *Esperanza Felix* were to be far more fortunate than they had ever dreamed. About the time the slaves were boarding the slave ship, two British warships, the *Mymidon* under the command of Captain Harry Leeke and the *Iphigenia*, commanded by Captain Meads, were sailing from Bathurst on anti-slavery patrol. The British Government had made slavery illegal in 1807 and since 1816 the British Navy patrolled the West African coast on the watch for slave trading ships.

It was a hot, sticky morning in 1821 when the lookout seamen on the *Mymidon* and the *Iphigenia* sighted the distant Portuguese sailing ship. The British ships at once went closer to investigate and were suspicious that it was a slave trader. The Portuguese captain was given the signal to stop and when he did so a party of British seamen went aboard. Their search soon revealed the large cargo of slaves.

In spite of the protests of the slave ship captain, all the slaves were assembled on the deck, ready for transfer to the British ships. The frightened people who had been dreading the voyage that was to take them into permanent slavery in Brazil, now found the impossible had happened. It was their captors who were being made prisoners while they were to be set free.

Adjai was completely puzzled when he was brought up from the hold of the ship into the sunshine and saw strange sailors walking about the deck. At first he could hardly believe what had happened. The sullen slave traders stood helpless while the Africans were taken off their ship. Adjai was put on board the *Mymidon*, still unsure what was going to happen to him.

To his surprise he was given his freedom to come onto the deck instead of being shut away in the hold of the ship. He became a great favourite of the British sailors because he was always willing to help and showed intelligence and good humour. Like all the boys on board, he was given food and clothing but he had to work.

The British warships were both well armed and able to deal with any slave ship that did not heed a warning to stop for a search. For some weeks the two ships sailed along the West African coast to complete their patrol before anchoring off the coast of Sierra Leone at the settlement of Freetown, which had been a British colony since 1808. By then thousands of freed slaves had settled there. Many of the rescued slaves on the *Mymidon* were put ashore to start a new life in Freetown.

There were often children on the slave ships and the Church Missionary Society had become concerned for their welfare. In 1814 the Society had built a home where these children could be looked after and educated. Adjai in fact seems to have had his first taste of freedom in the village of Bathurst near Freetown. Here he was met by a member of the Church Missionary Society.

Adjai could not have understood much of what was said to him, but he did know that everyone he met was friendly towards him. When he was sent to Mr and Mrs Davey, two missionary school-teachers, they did everything they could to make him feel happy and at home. There were new things to learn and to do which Adjai enjoyed very much. He was quick to learn from books and after a time he liked to hear stories read to him by Mr Davey from the Bible.

The Daveys had other Christian friends, Mr and Mrs Weeks, who also took an interest in Adjai. Adjai enjoyed making things from wood and Mr Weeks showed him how to do carpentry. Mrs Weeks was a teacher and willingly gave her time to help Adjai and a young girl ex-slave named Asano, to learn to read.

Life had taken some strange turns for Adjai. Instead of being sent as a slave to a strange land, he was now being well looked after and in spite of his suffering in recent months, he was soon able to settle in Bathurst. The white missionaries from other lands must have seemed strange to a young boy from Oshogun but they were kind to him and he had his freedom. And though far from his place of birth and his family, he was still in West Africa.

For years he lived in Bathurst and Mrs Weeks was delighted at the way he had learned to read all kinds of books including the Bible. He went regularly to the Christian church and on 11 December 1825, at the age of sixteen, he was baptised Samuel Adjai Crowther. In this way he retained his African name and took the name of Crowther from one of the founder members of the Church Missionary Society.

Mr and Mrs Davey often talked of returning to England for a visit. Then in the summer of 1826 they made plans to go on the voyage. At this time it was a slow journey in a sailing ship that had to brave the rough seas of the Atlantic Ocean.

"We have to go to London to attend meetings of the Church Missionary Society," Mr Davey told Adjai. "It will be many months before we return to Africa and we'd like you to come with us."

Adjai was delighted to be able to go on such a long voyage to a foreign land. In years to come he was to repeat this journey many times but the first occasion was the most exciting. After a voyage of some weeks, they landed in England on 16 August.

There was so much for Adjai to see and do in London. For a time, although he was seventeen years of age, he was able to go to the parochial school in Islington. Sometimes he visited the countryside. Everything was different from what he had known: the people, the buildings and the countryside. When winter came with its damp, cold fogs, Adjai wondered how people could be happy in such a climate.

It was the spring of 1827 when Adjai said

goodbye to all his new friends in England and sailed with the Daveys back to West Africa. In Sierra Leone a new college for the training of Christian priests had been opened in Freetown. It was called Fourah Bay College, and it was here that Adjai was to begin his studies in April of that year.

On his return there was one especially happy event for Samuel Crowther. He married Asano, the girl who had studied with him at Mr and Mrs Weeks. When she was baptised she had taken the name of Susan Thompson.

The new Head of Fourah Bay College was the Reverend Haensel who believed in strict discipline in both behaviour and work. Popular in England at that time was the monitor system of education where students were given extra responsibility in the school and called monitors. Four monitors were appointed at Fourah Bay and one of them was Samuel Adjai Crowther, the young married man of eighteen.

Samuel Crowther took easily to school discipline. He was intelligent and a natural hard worker. Most of the boys wore no shoes and very little clothing in the hot climate but Samuel came to the college wearing white stockings, a blue suit and a waistcoat. On Sundays he sometimes wore his beaver hat, possibly a souvenir of his visit to England.

Like the other boys, he did not care much for wearing shoes all the time but again his visit to England must have given him more practice in wearing shoes than the other students. However, when the Reverend Haensel told them that all the students were to wear shoes every Sunday when they attended the service at St George's Cathedral there was a problem. Noticing their glum expressions as they gazed at the shoes lined up by his desk, he pointed out that it was very important that as monitors they should set a good example.

"If the other boys see you in shoes, they too will wish to copy you," he said.

So the boys had to take the shoes away ready for the next visit to church on Sunday. One monitor named Attara was limping badly before they had even reached their dormitory.

"I am crippled already," he gasped, screwing up his face in pain. "How will I be able to walk three miles to the cathedral in such shoes as these?"

Somehow they had to find a way to wear the shoes. That evening they were in the dormitory practising walking in the shoes when the other boys returned. Far from wanting to copy the monitors, there were roars of laughter at the sight of them hobbling about and falling down in pain.

"You will all have to set out very early or you will be late to church," laughed one boy. "Although I doubt whether Attara will even get as far as the road."

Attara protested at this and made a desperate attempt to walk. He managed a few steps before he sat down and pulled off his shoes and flung them onto the floor.

"It's no good," he said. "I just can't walk with

them on my feet."

Then Samuel saw the humourous side of the situation. He managed to walk to the wall and then leaning against it, he started to walk. This way he kept his balance and did not have to put so much pressure on his feet. Although he could only make slow progress, his walk right round the dormitory in this way earned him the cheers and claps of the other boys.

On Sunday they had to set off for church in their shoes but nothing had changed to make them comfortable. They staggered along, stopping at regular intervals to sit on the ground and rest their feet. There was only one way they would ever get to church in the shoes. They agreed to take them off, walk almost to the church entrance and then quickly put on the shoes again.

When the church service was over, the monitors came out apparently wearing their new shoes proudly although in fact they were very uncomfortable. They were just waiting to find a quiet place where they could sit hidden from view and take them off. Then they set off as fast as they could for Fourah Bay College, putting the shoes on again just before they reached the College gates.

Every Sunday they repeated this and the Reverend Haensel was delighted to see his monitors setting such a good example to the other boys. Inevitably the day came when they did not change their shoes in time and were confronted by the College Head.

"Why are you not wearing your shoes today Samuel Crowther?"

Samuel was holding his shoes at that moment and thought it was useless to try to invent an excuse.

"I am sorry but these shoes hurt my feet so much that I can only walk properly without them," he said.

"You know I've told you that shoes must be worn in church and so I do not expect to see your bare feet," said the Reverend Haensel.

When on a subsequent Sunday the other monitors were caught without shoes the situation became serious. Then the boys heard about some boots that were for sale. They tried them on and although the boots squeaked, they were comfortable, so they bought them. The first Sunday they hurried into the dormitory to take off their boots before the other boys arrived, but to their surprise the boys envied them for possessing squeaky boots which became objects of pride.

Samuel was a devout Christian who wanted to be a missionary and a teacher when he left the college in two years time, when he would be twenty years old.

4

TEACHER AND MISSIONARY EXPLORER

"YOU try to do too much in one day," said Susan, his wife, when she noticed how tired Samuel was at the end of the day. "You should give yourself time when you can enjoy some rest."

"When I rest I like to study," said Samuel. "It will need a lot of time to master Greek and Latin. Perhaps one day I will follow a career in the Christian Church."

Samuel was working in a village school. Most of his lessons were taken outside, under the trees where there was shade. He had a small building where he kept his teaching equipment. Apart from teaching, he worked in the local Christian mission, taking prayers and Bible readings. He was always willing to do extra work if that was necessary and somehow he managed to find time to read Greek and Latin.

It was his village school though that probably took most of his time and thought. He knew that many of the children walked long distances from surrounding small villages to gain some kind of education in his school. He felt very strongly that it was his duty to do his very best for them and he set high standards of work and behaviour.

This was the beginning of his work as a missionary teacher in Africa. He regarded general learning through books and activities, where the children used their hands, as very important. He always had his Bible close at hand, too, and not a day passed without the children hearing readings from the Bible and saying Christian prayers.

Samuel Crowther as a young teacher soon had a reputation for being strict but fair. The children in his care both played and worked hard. In all this work he was helped and encouraged by his wife Susan. For five years he gained valuable experience and learnt the Christian needs of the people and their children in the country villages.

For much of the time, Samuel was teaching in the village of Regent where he often helped John Weeks, the missionary who had looked after him when he first arrived in Sierra Leone.

"Can you take prayers for me this Sunday?" asked John Weeks. "I have to be away for a few days."

"I'll do my best," said Samuel, "although I have to admit I feel nervous."

"Don't worry," laughed John Weeks. "I'm sure they enjoy listening to you more than they do me."

So that Sunday Adjai read the prayers and chose the hymns in the mission church. When John Weeks returned the following Sunday, he again let Adjai take the prayers. In his reports to the Church Missionary Society, he praised Adjai for all his help. Many prominent members of the

Society heard about the young African teacher who was always trying to improve his own education while at the same time he was a willing worker for Christianity.

Then in 1834, he received a letter offering him the chance to return to Fourah Bay College.

"You have already been a student at the college," said Susan. "Do you really want to give up teaching and start studying all over again?"

"This time I'm going to be a teacher at Fourah Bay," said Adjai. "It's certainly an opportunity I can't afford to miss. The students will be older and so I will have to do more advanced work with them. What's more, I will be able to do some studies of my own and improve my qualifications."

So he went to Fourah Bay College with his family and was happy and successful there as a teacher. His achievements were remembered by a small number of appreciative students and teachers. His life was to change suddenly, however, in 1841.

That year the Society for the Extinction of the Slave Trade sponsored an expedition of three ships to sail up the River Niger. The aim was to set up a model farm, to encourage trade and to make agreements with chieftains along the route where Christian missions would be built. It was hoped that if new trading centres could be established, the people living in these areas would not have the need to make a living from slave trading.

There were to be three ships: the *Albert*, the *Sudan* and the *Wilberforce*. There were 145 Europeans prepared to travel in the ships. Two missionaries would be needed. One of these was James Schon of the Church Missionary Society. He was originally from Germany, but had become a friend of Samuel Crowther whose name was suggested as the other missionary. Crowther seemed a good choice for he had already had some experience of travelling in Africa and had proved himself both as a missionary and teacher.

There was much about the expedition that appealed to Samuel and so when the offer came he accepted and left his post at Fourah Bay. Susan had always worked with her husband and helped him as much as possible but this time his work would mean separation from her and their growing number of children. She hoped the expedition would not be too dangerous and last too long.

"We shouldn't fear danger when the expedition is so worthwhile," he said. "I hope it won't last too long but of course we can never be sure exactly what will happen."

Not everyone in England thought the new expedition was a good idea. There were already many people who thought the founding of a settlement in Freetown would never work. When things went wrong in the early days of the settlement this had made them more critical. In spite of this, Prince Albert, the husband of Queen

37

Victoria, had attended a special celebration in London to mark the departure of the Europeans going with the expedition.

By July 1841 the three ships were ready to begin the journey up river. Crowther and Schon were on board to help and advise where necessary and to plan their new Christian missions. The majority of the Europeans must have needed advice for the journey, for they had little experience of the climate and conditions they would find.

First stop for the expedition was Cape Coast Castle. Here Crowther went ashore.

"If you have time you are very welcome to make use of the library," said Thomas Freeman who was head of the local church mission.

Samuel Crowther had already enjoyed Freeman's friendly hospitality and he always found great pleasure in browsing around libraries.

"While I am here, I must take the opportunity to have a look round this famous castle," said Samuel.

"Please do so," said Thomas Freeman. "While you are in the graveyard you will notice the stone in memory of Philip Quaque. He was an African who visited Britain some ninety years ago when he was a young man."

"I'll certainly look out for his gravestone," said Samuel. "I know that he was ordained a priest and returned to Africa to work for Christianity for more than fifty years."

Samuel Crowther was thirty-two years of age

at that time and although a teacher and a Christian worker, he was not yet a priest. If a man such as Philip Quaque could overcome all the difficulties of the eighteenth century, Samuel believed that he too could master the problems of Christian missionary work in nineteenth century Africa.

The first part of the journey was made without mishap. Captain Trotter, the ship's captain, made contact with chieftains' trading centres where much work would be done and there were good profits to be made. King Obi, one of the more important local rulers, was impressed and agreed to sign an agreement promising to abolish slavery in his land.

This was a good start and if other agreements could be made in this way, the leaders of the expedition would be delighted. Unfortunately though, those who had planned the expedition did not know enough about Africa. There were strange diseases and fevers and no one on the expedition knew the cause. Malaria is caused by mosquito bites but this fact was not known to travellers in Africa in 1841. The climate was hot and humid and the air was always full of large insects of all kinds. The people on board the ships, feeling desperately hot, wore as little clothing as possible. They had medicines with them but did not understand exactly what precautions they should take to avoid illness in the tropics.

After the successful meeting with King Obi, the expedition continued up river through a region that proved exceptionally unhealthy. Some people, especially the Europeans who were not used to the climate, became ill with fever. There was a supply of quinine on board that could have saved them if they had taken it before their illness. The sick people did not know this however, and the quinine, when it was taken at all, was used after the fever had started.

This was too late and some people died. The climate and conditions did not change and more travellers became ill with yellow fever and malaria. There was great distress on all three ships and even James Schon became very ill. Fortunately Samuel Crowther remained well, perhaps because he had grown up in West Africa and was used to the climate.

The situation worsened to the extent that there were more people both ill and dying with fever than there were fit and well.

For a time Captain Trotter did his best and kept the boats moving up river but it became obvious that the expedition was now a disaster. If he tried to go on, all lives might well be lost. So there had to come a moment when the decision was taken for the three boats to stop.

Everyone who was seriously ill was transferred to the *Sudan* and the *Wilberforce*. Reluctantly Captain Trotter ordered the two boats to go downstream back to their original base where they could receive proper medical attention.

Samuel Crowther continued in the *Albert* which Captain Trotter kept moving up river but there was now no hope of carrying out the aims of the expedition. Even on the *Albert* there were some sick people whose morale was low. They no longer had the strength to organise a series of trading centres. The model farm had been started but ended in failure. It was a dispirited group of travellers that eventually returned down the River Niger to go back to their homes.

More than a third of the people who had started with the expedition had died. James Schon had been fortunate to survive after serious illness. When he wrote his report to the Church Missionary Society, he praised Samuel Crowther for his contribution to the aims of the expedition and recommended that he should be considered for ordination as a Christian priest.

Susan Crowther and her children had hardly welcomed Samuel on his return from the ill-fated Niger expedition when there was talk of a journey to England in 1842. Apart from having to be away from his family, this would be an exciting journey, for the plan was that he would return at the end of the year as an ordained priest.

Samuel Crowther had made himself known to the Church Missionary Society through his all round ability as a missionary and the excellent journal he kept of his experiences when on the 1841 expedition up the River Niger. So in July 1842 he said goodbye to his family to fulfil the next stage of his career.

5

MORE DANGER FOR THE PRIEST

THE Church Missionary Society did not accept that the expedition of 1841 had been a complete failure. They had gained much very useful information from journals written by survivors such as Crowther. They had also agreed with James Schon that Africans could play an important part in the spreading of Christianity in West Africa.

In London Samuel had to go on a course of study at Islington Church College. It lasted for some months and at the end of it there was an examination which could have ended in failure. But Samuel Crowther had worked hard and this, coupled with his exceptional ability, brought him excellent results. He passed well and received his holy orders on 11 June 1843.

He still had some months to see and enjoy life in early Victorian London before he sailed for Africa in the late autumn. He would have experienced some very rough weather on his voyage back to West Africa at this time of the year but the Reverend Samuel Crowther had other things to think about. He was longing to see his family after such a long absence and his thoughts were on his new responsibilities as a priest.

Susan and his children met him at Freetown on Saturday, 2 December. There were also many friends to add to the welcome and to offer congratulations for his success. News of the arrival of a new African priest to preach at the mission church in Freetown caused a very large congregation to gather to hear him preach in Yoruba, his own language.

Samuel had already used his knowledge of this African language during the months that he was in England by writing and having published 'A Vocabulary of the Yoruba Language'. His ability to both preach in Yoruba and to translate the Bible into Yoruba was to play an important part in his Christian missionary work.

After so much separation from his family Samuel was glad to work near his own home. A year passed before he received a letter from Henry Townsend of the Church Missionary Society, asking him if he would be interested in going on an expedition with the German missionary, Herr Gollmer, to the town of Abeokuta.

About the year 1829 there had been warfare against the Egba people after an Egba chief had shot an Ife leader. The Egba had fled with other refugees to a region where they had founded a new town which they called Abeokuta, meaning the town under the rock. Sodeke, an Egba hunter, became the founder leader of Abeokuta, which had developed in importance until it now rivalled big towns such as Ibadan.

Members of the Church Missionary Society, such as Crowther's old friend Thomas Freeman, had already met Sodeke and found him sympathetic to the idea of a Christian mission in Abeokuta. Henry Townsend also visited Abeokuta and discussed with Sodeke the reception of a missionary party. Everything went well and Townsend sent letters to those he hoped would make up the party to depart on 18 December.

"This will mean that we have to be separated again," said Susan Crowther. "The letter gives the date of departure but no date for your return."

"Perhaps we can have this changed in some way," said Samuel. "I'll contact Herry Townsend and find out what can be done."

Susan was not very hopeful but eventually it was agreed that this time the Crowther family should not be split up for many months while Samuel was away. Instead the family would be able to travel to Abeokuta together. They spent Christmas Day in Monrovia, the chief town of Liberia, before travelling on to Badagri, which they reached on 17 January 1845.

Here the missionary party stayed while detailed plans were made for their departure on foot, through forest and open bush countryside to Abeokuta. It would be a hard journey but it was hoped that Sodeke would arrange for their safe passage and provide guides to bring them safely to their destination.

In some ways it was a strange experience for Samuel Crowther. He would be walking with his wife, his daughter Juliana and his son, Dandeson, and a party of friends through territory that more than twenty years before had been a place of fear. Not far away were the villages where he had stopped as a slave on his way to the coast.

At the beginning of 1845 it was the dry season. The missionary party could be on their way at any time. Then came a message that Sodeke had died and his successor, Sagbua, was unknown to the travellers. It was difficult to communicate with him and to know how they would be received if they made the journey. King Gezo of the Dahomey people was an enemy of the Yoruba and would be hostile to them. His armies were active and powerful in the land between Badagri and Abeokuta.

So the plans of the missionary party were postponed and it was decided to make Badagri a base until they could obtain accurate reports about the situation around Abeokuta. Samuel Crowther discussed what could be done while they were waiting with his German friend and fellow priest, Herr Gollmer.

There were two markets in Badagri where just about everything that was needed, from woven cloth to clay pots, could be bought. Between the markets stood a tree which gave welcome shade from the burning sun that shone day after day. As there was no church Crowther and Gollmer stood under the tree to preach to the people. As the weeks passed the small crowd they attracted at first grew into a large congregation.

"The time has come for us to open a mission church for the people of Badagri," said Crowther.

Gollmer agreed and a church was built that could accommodate the congregation of more than a hundred that gathered every Sunday. Samuel Crowther conducted his service in Yoruba and his experience as a teacher meant that he knew how to handle children and to make his Christian message interesting to them. By April, he was attracting forty children to the mission church every week.

Samuel always kept a diary and on 13 April he wrote, "The children seemed to be particularly delighted with the service and were heard distinctly joining in the Confession, the Lord's Prayer, the Creed and the Responses to the Ten Commandments in the Yoruba language."

Encouraged by the enthusiasm of the children, he opened a regular Sunday school which was a great success. Badagri, situated as it was on the coast, had grown up as an important centre of trade. There was a growing population and plenty to keep the members of the missionary party busy while they waited for the opportunity to set out for Abeokuta.

The years 1845 and 1846 passed however, and no decision was made. It seemed possible that the original idea for trading and mission stations in Abeokuta would have to be abandoned. However, the mission at Badagri was now going well and an experimental farm had been opened with a new steel corn mill. In addition mission schools had been opened.

At the end of the dry season in 1846 it was at last decided that they should set out for Abeokuta. The expedition seems to have been prepared inadequately for such a long and possibly dangerous journey. They had hardly got under way when rain clouds rolled overhead and they were swamped by devastating storms. There was some protection under the forest trees, and some of the party carried umbrellas, but with such driving rain, progress was slow and they were soon soaked.

As they trekked on, they had to keep a constant watch for wild animals and hostile villages who might attack them. Samuel must have wondered about Oshogun, his destroyed home town which was not far away from this region of the forest. At night they camped and tethered their horses but at first they did not come to any river and water supplies were a problem. So they laid out the large leaves from the tropical forest trees and caught enough water for their needs after every downpour.

It was not always possible to use the horses for riding as they slithered and slipped along the wet trails with loads of supplies and tents on their backs. Much of the time the Crowther family had to walk. For days there was little relief from the fierce storms and each evening they were exhausted. Then one night they reached a river bank, and pitched their tents for the night. Thunder and rain continued most of the night and in the morning Susan Townsend and her daughter went to the river to get water.

"The rain has made the river so deep it will not be possible for all of us to cross it," said Susan.

"We have to cross the river to reach Abeokuta," said Samuel, "so somehow a way across must be found."

The horses and supplies were taken across with men swimming by their side. Some supplies were lost but the task was carried out without any major disasters. But it was not so easy for the people who could not swim. Then somebody noticed that they had a bath tub. They found that it floated with someone sitting in it. So with one person sitting in the tub, two men waded into the water, holding the make-do boat on each side and pushed it across the river. And slowly, one by one, the members of the party reached the opposite river bank.

Travel through the forest remained dangerous and difficult. Day after day, the storms raged with constant thunder and lightning, heavy rain and gusts of wind bent trees so that they snapped. Because of this the forest was littered with fallen trees and broken branches.

The travellers made detours round the tree trunks, only for the horses to get stuck in thick, wet, slippery mud, hidden under long grass. For some way, Susan Crowther travelled in a hammock carried by two men but they fell so often that in the end she had to walk. Then a horse would slip and fall and have to be reloaded. In the meantime some other accident would occur.

As they approached Abeokuta however, their

spirits rose. They had come up against constant obstacles and serious difficulties but had overcome them. They were tired and longing for rest but at least there had been no hostile attacks. Now they felt a growing confidence that they would complete their journey successfully. With their final destination not far away, they were met by guides, sent out by King Sagbua, to welcome them. At last they rode through the gates of Abeokuta, drenched to the skin by the tropical rain.

This town of the Egba people was a big place with an army of 15,000 warriors. Fortunately for the weary party of travellers, King Sagbua was friendly and generous with his hospitality. They in turn gave him a gift from England. Sagbua offered to pay some of the costs of building a church after Samuel Crowther had explained the many benefits the mission would bring to the town.

"You can have land," Sagbua told Crowther. "Some of my people will help you to build the mission."

Samuel was delighted with this offer. As soon as the missionary party had settled into their new homes, they set to work. With Egba women helping with the collection of clay for the walls, a mission church soon took shape. When it was finished, Crowther had his centre for Christian activities.

For a time, as was usual with him, he was completely absorbed with his work. Sometimes people from the nearby town of Abake visited the markets of Abeokuta to buy and sell goods. Occasionally they visited the Christian church. One Sunday an elderly lady from Abake came to the mission church for the first time. As she listened to the sermon her eyes filled with tears. It was Crowther's mother, Afala.

At the end of the service Afala went to her son but for some minutes she was speechless with emotion. Then with a great effort, she managed to explain who she was and that she now lived at Abake.

"It is wonderful to see my Adjai, alive and well after all these years," she said as she embraced him.

Samuel looked at her in amazement. Now it was his turn to be overcome with the joy of seeing his mother again and he too could only stand and hug her, unable to speak and tell her of his delight at having met her again. When at last she could talk, his mother explained how she and her daughters had been slaves for many years. It wasn't until one of her daughters had been able to save enough money to buy their freedom that they had eventually settled in Abake.

Now she came to live with Samuel Crowther and his family. There was another wonderful moment to come for them both. On 5 February 1848 Afala attended her son's service at the Abeokuta Mission Church and there he baptised her a Christian. They were able to enjoy some happy times in Abeokuta. But changes were on the way, bringing dangers and terrible wars.

6

THE ATTACK ON ABEOKUTA

THE horseman galloping in the gate of Abeokuta was from Isiaga, an Egbado town to the north of Abeokuta. He brought a message of warning. Isiaga had been attacked and captured by an army of 16,000 from Dahomey. The leader of Isiaga known as the Oba did not have an army strong enough to fight the Dahomeyans and so he had surrendered to them.

The Oba was asked by the Dahomeyan leaders which part of the walls of Abeokuta would be the easiest to attack and he told them the south-west. Then he sent his messenger in secret to Abeokuta, alerting them to prepare for the coming attack. The people of Abeokuta at once set about repairing and building up their town walls, especially the south-west section and the Egba army of Abeokuta was put on battle alert.

When the news reached the members of the Christian mission, they were very concerned. They had been in contact with the British consul in that part of Africa, John Beecroft, for some time and as a result he had arranged for guns and ammunition to be sent to the mission. These were in turn issued to the Egba army.

In March 1851 the army of Dahomey assembled before Abeokuta and demanded surrender which was refused. The attacking army was unusual as it included some 6,000 women fighters, known as Amazons. The Dahomey warriors launched their attack on the south-west wall but were beaten off. They came again, this time attempting to climb the wall but found that far from it being a weak spot, it was well defended.

In the meantime other Dahomey warriors were attacking the main gate of Abeokuta. The Egba army went out to meet them but had to retreat. There was a real danger that the attackers would get into Abeokuta and take over the town. The Egba, armed with the guns and ammunition issued to them by the people at the mission station fought back with great determination, causing heavy casualties to the Dahomeyans.

For three years the mission at Abeokuta, with its church and schools, had been a centre of Christian teaching in this region of Africa. Now as the battle raged, there was a danger that everything that had been built up with so much effort could be destroyed.

Samuel Crowther tried to encourage those who came to him in fear. It would be a strange turn of events if, after escaping from slavery so many years ago, he and his family were captured and sold again. It was known that not so many years before, the Dahomeyans had attacked the town of Otta and sold all its people into slavery.

The messages coming through from those defending the walls of Abeokuta, however, were increasingly hopeful. The attackers were suffering terrible losses in their constant efforts to scale the walls of the town. Sensing victory, the army of Abeokuta made a decisive attack on their enemies and drove them off. The King of Dahomey realising at last that his army was in danger of total defeat withdrew his surviving warriors to their own territory.

Abeokuta had been saved. The work of the missionaries had made the town well known, even in England. There was therefore great concern when people read in their newspapers that a war was going on in this region of Africa. Samuel Crowther received anxious messages enquiring about the fate of the mission. He was glad to be able to report that the mission and the missionaries had survived but he had been greatly saddened by the terrible loss of human life and the thousands of wounded that had resulted from the battles for the town.

One message from Lord Palmerston expressed a wish to help the people of Abeokuta as much as possible. Lord Palmerston invited Crowther to come to London to explain the urgent needs of the people and mission of Abeokuta. It was an opportunity not to be missed and this time there would be no separation. Samuel Crowther was to be accompanied to England by his wife and family.

7

A VISIT TO ENGLAND

BY August that year the Crowther family had arrived in England. Although it was summer, the weather seemed unusually cool to the African family. The Crowther family found they needed different clothes to feel comfortable in the English climate. The traffic of London too was an amazing sight to Susan Crowther and her son and daughter. There were so many carriages and carts of all sizes that even crossing the road could be dangerous. Everything they saw was strange and interesting to them.

For Samuel Crowther it was a chance to talk about Africa and its problems to the Prime Minister, members of his Government and even Queen Victoria and her husband, Prince Albert. One day Lord John Russell, the Prime Minister, came to see the Crowther family.

"As you know Prince Albert takes a great interest in the work of the Christian missions in West Africa," he said. "He invites you to come to see him at Windsor Castle to discuss the progress that is being made and in particular the needs that you have at Abeokuta."

So on the afternoon of 18 November, Crowther and Lord John Russell arrived at Windsor Castle. Before he had time to be nervous, Crowther found himself standing in a beautiful room, talking to Prince Albert who produced a map of West Africa and began to ask him questions about it. The conversation was friendly and Samuel Crowther quickly felt at ease.

As it was a gloomy November afternoon, the light was not good and it was not easy to see the details on the map. While Lord John Russell was talking to the prince, a lady entered and commented that they needed a lamp. This was soon brought in by a servant and Crowther showed the prince on this map, the position of Lagos and other ports.

For some time they talked about the slave trade and Crowther's experience of being rescued from slavery. All the time the lady just listened while Prince Albert and Crowther turned the pages of the atlas. They discussed the work at the mission station in Abeokuta, and as a page was turned the draught caught the flame in the lamp and put it out. For a moment they stood in near darkness. Then Prince Albert, who had been looking at the position of Abeokuta, spoke to the lady.

"Would Your Majesty kindly bring us a candle from the mantelpiece?"

The lady did as she was asked and with the candle lit, the Prince resumed his interest in the map, but Crowther could no longer concentrate. The words "your majesty" echoed in his mind. He suddenly realised that the small lady standing quietly next to them was Queen Victoria. It was with some difficulty that he gathered his thoughts and continued to discuss West Africa.

The prince explained to the queen some of Crowther's achievements as a teacher and Christian missionary in Africa. He especially spoke of his work providing the people with the Bible translated into Yoruba. Queen Victoria was most interested to hear this and asked Crowther to say the Lord's Prayer in Yoruba.

Speaking quietly but clearly Crowther said the prayer with the queen and Prince Albert listening attentively. At the end the queen smiled and was obviously delighted.

"That was most pleasant," she said. "Yoruba is a soft and melodious language."

The queen and her husband had shown a genuine concern for the progress of Christianity and education in West Africa. Crowther hoped his talk with the royal couple would create more interest in England in the work of the Abeokuta mission.

One of his finest memories during this visit to England was of a meeting with Sir Harry Leeke. Crowther had been working on a Yoruba translation at the Church Missionary House in London when he recognised the Englishman standing nearby. Crowther introduced himself as the young Adjai of 1821 who had been rescued by the *Mymidon*.

"I remember the occasion well," Sir Harry Leeke told him. "How good it is to see you again after so many years."

The two men had a long talk and as a result of this chance meeting, Samuel Crowther was invited to be a guest at Sir Harry Leeke's country home. He accepted the invitation and while he was there took the opportunity to preach in the local church.

Crowther was also invited to be a guest of the students at Cambridge University. He gave them a talk about conditions in West Africa, especially describing what was being done in the Niger missions. He ended by appealing to the university students to do what they could to help. If possible some of them should come out to West Africa to share in the Christian work that was already going on there.

By the time he left England with his family in December 1851, Samuel Crowther could look back on a visit of great interest and achievement. He had met some of the most important people in the country and everywhere he went he had been listened to with respect. In addition he had been able to renew old friendships and make new ones.

On their return to West Africa, Crowther and his family visited Freetown and Lagos. As always he kept a diary and after his stay in Lagos he wrote, "I went over the spots where slaves used to be. What a difference now. Some of the spots are now converted into plantations of maize and cassava. Sheds built on others are filled with casks of palm oil and other merchandise, instead of slaves in chains and irons, in agony and despair."

There was no easy way for the Crowther family to get back to the mission at Abeokuta. After their stay in Lagos, they had to prepare to make the long trek through the forest and bush country to reach their destination. Samuel Crowther was not sorry to leave the place where thirty years before he had stood in a slave market and had been forced to board a slave ship.

It was by then June 1852 and still the dry season, so the Crowther family set off before the rains started. Fortunately they were all seasoned travellers and this time they managed to make the journey without either accidents or illness.

When they saw the high rocks of Abeokuta, towering up in the distance, they knew that their journey was at last at an end. It was good to be back again and to be met and welcomed by their friends. There was so much to talk about that Susan Crowther thought she would never finish.

"The first thing I must do is to check on the mission church building," said Samuel. "It was in need of repair when I left here."

"The first thing you must do is to rest," laughed Susan. "I'm sure the mission church has been well looked after."

Samuel was able to tell the other missionaries of his discussions in England which he hoped would result in much needed aid. Apart from his work at the mission church Samuel spent much of his time making translations into Yoruba of parts of the Old Testament. When these were finished he made copies available to the missions. He always kept a careful record of his work and for many years he sent regular reports to the Church Missionary Society in London. The Atlantic could be very rough, especially in the Bay of Biscay, so Crowther's reports sometimes took many months to reach their destination.

The situation was about to improve, however, through the efforts of a Liverpool merchant, Macgregor Laird. There were growing trading opportunities in the Niger Delta and along the Niger River. To encourage traders to go to West Africa, the British Government needed a fleet of modern steamers and the responsibility for providing these was given to Macgregor Laird.

For years Laird had been interested in the trading prospects in West Africa. Now, in 1852, he owned and supplied an efficient fleet that gave a good service between England and the coastal settlements of West Africa. Hundreds of British companies began to operate in the Niger Delta. People such as Samuel Crowther, who needed to keep in contact with London, now had a faster and more efficient mail service.

During 1854 the British Government, hoping to increase trade, gave a contract to Laird to build and equip a steamer to take an expedition up the Rivers Niger and Benue. Although he was now over sixty years of age, John Beecroft was chosen to lead this expedition into unknown territory. He needed others of suitable courage and experience to go with him. Such a man was Samuel Crowther.

8

MORE EXPEDITIONS

JOHN BEECROFT had been Britain's Consul for the Bights of Benin and Biafra since 1849. By then he had already seen much of West Africa, worked for the abolition of the slave trade and looked after the welfare of liberated slaves. He had explored thousands of miles of Africa along the Cross and Niger rivers, visited Abeokuta and met missionaries there, including Samuel Crowther.

In 1854, Beecroft with the surgeon-consul, William Baikie, were planning their expedition up river in Macgregor Laird's new steamer, the *Pleiad*. After going up the Rivers Niger and Benue, they hoped to reach Lake Chad, explore the region, make trading agreements and contact two European explorers who had been missing for some time. They were Heinrich Bath, a German and another explorer named Vogel.

For such a long journey into unknown territory, Beecroft had needed a surgeon and naturalist and was fortunate to find a man of outstanding ability in William Baikie. Of course other specialists were needed for the expedition, including African helpers and missionaries.

At that time Samuel Crowther was back in Abeokuta, happy with his family and absorbed

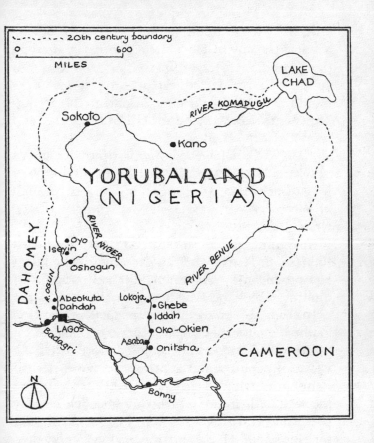

- - - 20th century boundary

0 ———— 600
MILES

LAKE
CHAD

RIVER KOMADUGU

Sokoto

Kano

YORUBALAND
(NIGERIA)

DAHOMEY

RIVER NIGER

RIVER BENUE

Oyo
Iseyin
Oshogun

R. OGUN

Abeokuta
Dahdah
LAGOS
Badagri

Lokoja

Ghebe
Iddah
Oko-Okien

Asaba
Onitsha

CAMEROON

Bonny

N

with his Christian missionary work both in and around the town. He returned to his home one day to find a letter waiting for him from Captain John Beecroft. It requested him to go to Fernando Po to join an expedition up the Rivers Niger and Nun with the aim of exploring the land around Lake Chad.

"Why do you have to go at this time when there is so much to do here?" Asked Susan.

"I don't have to go, but it's an exceptional opportunity to spread Christianity to new lands."

So Samuel set off for Fernando Po to go aboard the *Pleiad*. It was a new steamer with the latest equipment and William Baikie had supplies of quinine which he issued to all members of the expedition every day. This medical precaution had a very good effect on everyone's health.

Crowther had met Beecroft before when he visited Abeokuta and admired the work he had done in Africa over the years. An exciting journey with many worthwhile discoveries, lay ahead if everything went well. The *Pleiad* headed for the Niger Delta and was making good progress when there was sudden tragedy.

John Beecroft, who was over sixty years of age, became ill. His condition worsened and in spite of everything that William Baikie, as a doctor, could do for him, he died. Everyone in the expedition was shocked and Samuel Crowther felt as if he had lost a friend. He wrote in his diary, "It will be a long time before his place can be taken by another who will have the same interest in the country and its people as he did."

It seemed that the expedition, now without an experienced leader like Beecroft, might have to be abandoned. In this moment of crisis, William Baikie proved to be a man of exceptional ability and courage. He had a great love of Africa and was an explorer of the finest type. Suddenly and unexpectedly he found himself responsible for the expedition.

"We are going ahead as planned," he informed his fellow travellers. "The *Pleiad* will continue its journey up the Niger and I know I can rely on your help."

Samuel Crowther was glad that the expedition was not to be abandoned. Certainly he would do everything that he could to ensure its success. At every stopping point, he was invaluable with his knowledge of the local languages. Whenever possible he took the opportunity to meet the local chieftains and explained the benefits that the expedition could bring to their people.

Of course the Christian message of the Bible would be explained to the chief. Then the possibilities of future visits by Christians would be discussed and the chief would agree that he would have a mission in his village. Finally Crowther gave him some Christian tracts that had been translated into Yoruba so that the chief could show these to his people.

These meetings that Crowther had with village chiefs established friendly feeling between the villagers and the travellers. When William Baikie came ashore, the chief was usually prepared to listen to him and to discuss trade and give useful information about the local area.

At the end of September, they arrived at a village called Dulti. Baikie was amazed to find the village built in the river and all the inhabitants were walking about with water up to their knees. With another traveller named Mr May, William Baikie went in a canoe paddled by his team of Africans, known as krumen, to have a closer look at the village. It was a dangerous thing to do and the *Pleiad* expedition nearly lost its second leader. The amazing sight of Dulti village, however, had made Baikie careless over his safety.

"Just look at that child," he shouted as they approached the buildings above the water. A child was wading towards them up to his waist but seeing they were strangers, he turned and made for his house.

The people of Dulti had learned that strangers often meant trouble and did not welcome them. They therefore viewed the approach of a strange canoe with a mixture of fear and anger. Canoes of warriors were soon heading menacingly in Baikie's direction.

"Turn round," yelled Baikie as ten canoes came towards them at full speed. "Get back to the *Pleiad*!"

The African krumen realised the danger and paddled the canoe with all their strength back towards the ship. They were hopelessly outnumbered by their pursuers who, if they could get close enough, would show them no mercy.

Fortunately for Baikie and May, their krumen showed great skill. What afterwards became known as the great Dulti chase, now took place. At one moment the Dulti canoes seemed to be closing, only for Baikie's men to make a supreme effort and just keep ahead. At last they came up to their ship. Everyone from the canoe scrambled aboard and the warriors from Dulti, satisfied that they had driven the intruders away, returned to their village.

There were other situations where the local people were suspicious of the arrival of the expedition. It could have been dangerous in Gandiko when Ama, the chief, threatened to attack. Samuel Crowther went ashore and risked his life to talk to the chief. He was able to persuade Ama to accept them in peace and friendship.

Although the expedition heard rumours about Barth and Vogel, the missing explorers could not be found. In other ways, though, there were great achievements. Trading opportunities were improved and new missions would be opened as a result of Crowther's efforts. In addition all kinds of new discoveries had been made about the people and the country up river. One great success, compared with the previous river journey that Crowther had made, was that this time Baikie had taken wise medical precautions and fewer people suffered from malaria and yellow fever. The one sadness of the expedition had been the death of John Beecroft.

When they returned safely to the coast at the

end of their journey, everyone assembled on deck and Samuel Crowther conducted a service of thanksgiving. William Baikie realised the great value of having an African priest such as Crowther on an expedition up river. He thanked him for everything that he had done, saying that much of their success was due to Crowther's work and ability.

It was to be expected that when William Baikie again led another expedition up the Niger, this time hoping to reach Kano, Sokoto and Rabba, he would invite Samuel Crowther to join him. It was 1857 and the expedition was due to leave Fernando Po on 29 June. This time there was no question of taking his family, but there would be opportunities to open Christian missions in Onitsha and there would be another freed African slave, the Reverend Taylor, travelling with the party.

"I hope to be back soon," Samuel told Susan, who was in Lagos with their children. "But of course we can't be sure when that will be."

"The main thing is that you return safely," she said. "This will be such a long journey that I can't believe that I will see you again soon."

She knew her husband could not resist the challenge to spread Christianity whenever the chance came along, whatever the risks or the time involved. It might be a year rather than a few months, and she had come to accept this, but she did not realise that it would be two and a half years before Samuel would return.

The boat was the *Dayspring* and the aim of the expedition, as it had been in the past, was to start up both trading and mission stations. Simon Jonas and others with a commission from the Church Missionary Society to found the Niger Mission, were with Crowther and Taylor. At the riverside town of Onitsha, Taylor and Jonas went ashore and stayed to build a new mission station.

Samuel Crowther also went ashore to check what needed to be done. He was especially concerned about the poor condition of the local people who seemed to be making little effort to improve their lives. Crowther suggested that once the mission was built, crops such as cassava, Indian corn and fruit trees could be grown on the surrounding ground. The local people should be encouraged to grow their own crops.

There were some dangerous incidents later on when any member of the expedition might have been killed. Crowther had successfully started Christian missions at Gbebe and Lokoja and was planning to do the same at Jebba, a town of growing importance. The river at this point flowed very fast and there were dangerous rocks, including a rock called the Juju rock. This proved too much for the hull of their ship which was torn apart on the rock.

It was the rainy season and the weather was bad. As their boat started to sink, everyone on board grabbed what supplies they could and scrambled into canoes. They all reached land safely but they lost their ship. It looked as though they would have to make their way overland in a season of constant heavy rain with all the hardship this would mean.

The members of the expedition made a camp. After some days they were short of food and had to search for wild honey and corn. There were many dangers. In the wet grass under the trees there was always the risk of snakes and as the camp became established they were troubled by wild beasts foraging for food. However with Dr. Baikie to advise the travellers on how to look after their health, they survived until October 1858 when another river steamer, the *Sunbeam*, came to rescue them.

"I would like to stay ashore a while at Onitsha," Samuel Crowther told Dr. Baikie on their return journey. "I must see what Taylor and Jonas have managed to do with the new mission."

"Thank you for all your excellent help," said Baikie. "We wish you a safe journey and I will see you again in either Lagos or Abeokuta."

Crowther went to the mission in Onitsha and found that a school had been opened and was well attended. The mission had been built and that too was a success. Although in future years it was to face attacks, in the end the Onitsha mission station was one of the most successful in the region.

When he left Onitsha, Crowther faced the last stage of his journey. He went first by canoe to Idda and then on to Rabbah. From here he set out for the town of Ilorin where he was welcomed by the king. After enjoying the hospitality of this town, he again began an overland trek to Abeokuta. It was not a good time for travel as there was a constant risk of fighting between various towns. Abeokuta and Ilorin were allies with other towns against Ibadan and Oyo.

In spite of the dangers, Crowther reached Abeokuta safely and found Dr. Baikie already there. After a short stay here, Crowther went to Lagos to rejoin his family from whom he had been separated for two and a half years. Over the years Samuel Crowther had risked his life to travel this region of West Africa and set up as many Christian missions as possible. As he went with traders, usually the trading stations grew up alongside the missions. Both were constantly threatened by war.

Crowther's family had become used to the fact that he would always be prepared to go off on some long journey, either overland or up river, to spread the ideas of Christianity. His translations of the Bible into Yoruba and his Yoruba dictionary were both valuable aids for Christianity and education. But by March 1860 there was war in Yorubaland and this made travel for missionaries such as Crowther impossible.

For years the missions that Crowther had created inland were left to struggle on alone. No one could be sure that they had not been destroyed in the fighting that was going on as boats from the coast would not dare sail up river in case of attack. Travel on foot was far too dangerous and during this time Samuel Crowther had to stay with his family and work with the local Christian mission. Of course he would be off at the first opportunity but the next long journey he was to undertake was to London.

9

THE FIRST BISHOP OF WEST AFRICA

WHEN a letter arrived for Samuel Crowther, his wife usually assumed that it was some request for him to travel far away to a mission station. The letter that arrived one morning in 1864, was something different however.

"No, I'm not going exploring again," he smiled when he had read the letter. "This time they want me to go to London. It's from Henry Venn. He wants me to attend a special meeting of the Committee of the Church Missionary Society."

"When do they want you to go?"

"I'm afraid it's very soon. They want me to make sure I'm in England in time for the meeting."

Henry Venn was secretary of the Church Missionary Society and had always believed that African Christians were needed to spread Christian ideas in Africa. In this he was following up Schon's advice that Africans would be more suitable for expeditions of exploration than would Europeans who were not used to the climate and conditions. For the same reason

Venn believed it would be better to appoint an African as Bishop of West Africa rather than a European. The man he had in mind was Crowther.

Not realising the true reason for his visit and having so little time to prepare, Crowther was still wearing his usual plain old coat with a row of brass buttons when he sailed for England. The Atlantic was always liable to be rough but by now he was used to the voyage in spite of its storms.

In London, he was met by Henry Venn and taken to the meeting. Here he was questioned about his work and he explained the difficulties of organising Christian missions at such places as Onitsha and Abeokuta. As he started to speak somebody was rude enough to laugh. Crowther showed no sign of anger. He realised what they thought was funny and he indicated his old coat.

"As you can see, so that I would not be late for this appointment I had to leave Africa in a hurry," he said. "This old coat of mine is the one I wear when I tour my Christian missions and I had just been on such a tour when I had to leave and come to London. You may find it amusing but I find it practical for my work and at the moment I'm afraid it is the only one I have."

Crowther then went on to explain the needs of his missions. At the top of his list were more missionaries but he also warned of the difficulties they would have to face if they came to West Africa. Henry Venn thanked him for his interesting survey of the situation.

"What we really need in West Africa is someone who can be the leader of the Christian Church," he said. "That person should in our opinion be a bishop and because of your ability, experience and achievements, we are going to recommend you to be Bishop of West Africa."

Samuel Crowther was overwhelmed at Venn's announcement. His immediate reply was to say that he was not worthy of such a high appointment in the Church. He needed time to think about taking this unexpected responsibility. His old friend James Schon was in London and Crowther went to see him and told him of the offer that had been made to him. Schon had no doubt that he should accept and become the first African bishop of this region.

So Crowther returned to Henry Venn and agreed to accept the high office of bishop. On 29 June 1864, at the age of fifty-four, he attended the special ceremony at Canterbury Cathedral, to be consecrated Bishop of West Africa. Admiral Harry Leeke was one of the large crowd of people in the cathedral. He was the man who was in many ways responsible for such a ceremony being possible. Also his old teacher Mrs Weeks, was present.

News of his appointment reached West Africa and when he arrived in Freetown in August, crowds were waiting to welcome their first African bishop. It was a very exciting moment for him, and fitting that he should go straight to Fourah Bay College where he had been both student and teacher. In his student days the College had been a place for training village teachers. In 1845 money had been raised to build a new four storey building and since then the education had been for future missionaries.

Bishop Crowther, now an honoured guest at the College, was interested to note that Greek, Hebrew and Arabic were all being taught to the new generation of students. There was already talk of making the College into a university but this was not to happen for many years.

Once back in West Africa the new bishop soon set to work on the organisation of new missions. Very often he joined in himself, especially if children were involved. At Gbebe, while he stayed at the mission station, he took the children's Sunday school class every week and always greatly enjoyed it.

The Port of Bonny had long been a slave trading centre from which thousands of slaves were shipped across the Atlantic. A very large British naval force patrolled the seas of this region and slave trading was eventually stopped. The people of Bonny then became busy with trade in palm oil, but there was no Christian mission station there in the 1860s. This was a challenge to Bishop Crowther.

When he arrived in Bonny to start the first Delta Mission, he found there were two main problems. First it was the rainy season and the whole place was flooded. No matter how hard the bishop searched there seemed to be no suitable spot where a mission station could be built. He was looking for a dry, firm site for a permanent building that would not be flooded every year.

Not far from Bonny he discovered a high, sandy stretch of ground that would provide the right foundations for the building.

The second big problem was of a different nature. The people of Bonny worshipped the monitor lizard which was a giant among lizards. Because it was regarded as sacred no lizard was ever harmed. The result was that there were monitor lizards everywhere. They crawled about the streets, into houses, and no doubt would crowd into the new Christian mission house when it was completed.

When he was in Bonny in 1867, Bishop Crowther visited the town chief. Crowther persuaded him that the monitor lizards were becoming a pest and should no longer be worshipped as sacred creatures. The chief agreed and from April that year the worship of the lizards had to stop. The unfortunate reptiles were now regarded as creatures to be hunted and killed and it soon became rare to see one there. In the meantime the mission was built to establish interest in Christianity.

Since the middle of the nineteenth century there had been a steady growth of Christian missions in West Africa, many of them inspired by Bishop Crowther. Through the years he had produced books intended to help the people to understand the Bible in their own language and to help those who wished to study African languages. Apart from his Yoruba dictionary, there was his Grammar and Vocabulary of the Nupe Language published in 1864.

It was encouraging to see real progress in Christian teaching taking place at the missions but there was always the danger that all the effort could come to nothing. The same year that Bishop Crowther had gone to Bonny, messages of war arrived against the town of Gbebe which had a small mission station. The Basses and Akiaias people attacked Gbebe and a battle took place which ended with the capture of the town.

The British Consul, William Fell, showed great bravery by leading a rescue operation. Many Christians were taken by canoes to Lokoja to receive hospitality at the mission station there. The town of Gbebe was burnt down, including the Christian mission and many people lost their lives in the fighting.

It was not long after this that the Bishop nearly lost his life. Bishop Crowther's son Dandeson was now a young man who sometimes accompanied his father on missionary journeys. In September 1867 they went on such a journey by canoe.

Also in their party was Mr. Moore, a mission builder. They were going to visit mission stations including the one in the town of Idah. Travelling across country on foot was so slow, difficult and dangerous, that Bishop Crowther made use of the river whenever he could. Whatever method of travel was used, it was not a good time for either traders or missionaries. There was growing conflict between the people of Abeokuta and Lagos and other towns, and strangers arriving in any town or village were not likely to be welcome.

Bishop Crowther and his son, Dandeson, came as friends who knew most of the chieftains in the villages and towns by the river bank. This time however, they did not receive the friendship they expected. They reached a village called Oko-Okien and as Crowther knew the chief, Abokko, he went ashore to greet him. When he reached the chief's hut, he expected Abokko to come out to welcome him but he did not.

When he entered the hut, the bishop found Abokko in an angry mood, shouting about traders who never brought him gifts when they passed his village in their boats. He then demanded gifts from the bishop and when there were none he stalked from the hut.

Bishop Crowther was about to return to the canoe when he noticed that Abokko's men were attacking Dandeson, Mr Moore and his crew. Abokko was calling to them to take all of the supplies from the canoe and bring them into the village. As the bishop's men were outnumbered, he called to them not to fight, knowing only too well that they might all be killed. So the supplies were taken to Chief Abokko's hut and the bishop and his party were left with nothing.

When Bishop Crowther went to see Abokko, he found him sitting outside his hut, obviously quite pleased with the stolen goods that had come his way.

"Why do you steal my supplies which are

necessary for our journey when I have never done anything to harm you?" demanded the bishop.

"You have done nothing against me but the merchants who pass my village, leave me nothing. Why do you not order them to give me the presents which are my right?"

"Because I sail in the ships of the traders that does not mean I own the ships," said the bishop. "I am concerned only with the Christian mission stations."

Abokko was in a strange and ugly mood. Far from accepting the bishop's explanation, he began to make new demands.

"You are all my prisoners," he said. "You can only go free when the traders load three of their ships with gifts for me."

"I cannot ask them to do that," said the bishop. "When I travel in their boats I am only a passenger. The boats belong to the traders and not to me."

For some time he tried to make Abokko see reason but the chief was in no mood to listen. In the end the bishop and all his party were forced into a dirty old hut with nowhere to sleep but a wet and muddy floor. Guards were put on duty outside the hut to ensure that none of the prisoners could escape.

This situation continued for some nights and some of the canoe boatmen in the bishop's party became restless and angry. They wanted to fight the guards and attempt to escape and would have done so if the bishop had not stopped them. In the end one of the guards bullied a boatman and shouted at him. When the boatman answered back the guard struck him. Immediately four other boatmen came to his aid and pushed the guard away.

This was not the end of the matter. The guard reappeared with a large number of other guards, overpowered the four boatmen and put them in chains. Bishop Crowther protested strongly against this act of cruelty but the guards ignored him. In Abokko's village there was one man among a number of slaves who hated the chief. When he had the opportunity he tried to do little kindnesses for the bishop such as bringing him extra food and clothing for warmth.

On 23 September, the day before Dandeson's birthday, Bishop Crowther wrote a message asking for help. He gave it to the slave and asked him to try to get it to King Atta of Iddah. The man promised to do his best.

Dandeson's twenty-fourth birthday was spent in the prison hut. They all knew that they survived on the whim of Chief Abokko. At any time his patience could run out and he would order them to be put to death. Unhappy to see his son spending his birthday in this way, the bishop wrote in his diary, "How different was this from his former birthday, kept among his relatives and friends who congratulated and wished him many happy returns."

One day Abbega, the special messenger of the British Consul, arrived at the village. He met Abokko, who demanded a ransom of a thousand bags of cowrie shells that had to be delivered to him before he would release the prisoner. Bishop Crowther also saw Abegga and gave him a message for the Consul.

More days passed with the bishop and his party still held as prisoners. Then one morning they could hear the sound of a steamboat chugging past Oko-Okien. On board was Colonel Rolleston and the British Consul, William Fell.

The prisoners were not sure what was happening. The engine of the steamer went quiet, followed by the sound of footsteps and people's voices outside their hut. Someone pushed open the door and shouted to them to run towards the river bank where a canoe was waiting to take them to the steamer. They ran for their lives and reached safety without injury. William Fell had tried to argue with Abokko before turning to run for the canoe. Before he could get away, he was hit by a poisoned arrow. Fell was helped into the canoe and taken aboard the steamer, *Thomas Bazely*, but he died as they approached Lokoja.

King Atta of Iddah, an ally of Abokko, threatened the lives of the missionaries in his town. Because of the difficulty of reaching Iddah, Bishop Crowther decided not to risk the lives of his missionary workers there. He therefore reluctantly closed down the mission station in Iddah. This was a result of the disastrous journey with his son Dandeson.

Dandeson Crowther had survived an adventure with his father where either could have lost his life. Like his father, he was a devoted Christian. They were to work together for many years on the Niger mission. Two of Bishop Crowther's daughters married Christian priests but his other son, Josiah, eventually became a businessman in Freetown.

When in 1870, Bishop Crowther went to London to visit the headquarters of the Church Missionary Society, he took Dandeson with him. His son's record as both a student and a missionary worker was good enough for the Society to recommend that he should be ordained a priest. It was a great pleasure for Bishop Crowther to be able to carry out the ceremony of ordination at St Mary's Church, Islington.

They returned to a West Africa still troubled by wars. One of the main difficulties faced by Bishop Crowther in keeping his Christian missions working well was the frequent conflict between the leaders of the towns. The main routes into the interior were always threatened, which made communication with the mission stations a constant risk. There was warfare between Ibadan and the Egba and very little opportunity for trade between the various towns.

If he could not travel inland to visit his missions, then Bishop Crowther had other work to do. He was always busy on Yoruba translations of the Bible and prayers. Then there were the Christian missions along the coast and in the Niger Delta. They needed his attention and very often when he visited them, he was accompanied by his son, now the Reverend Dandeson Crowther.

10

THE CHRISTIAN WORK
GOES ON

"IT'S the boat we have always wanted," said Bishop Crowther as he looked at the new paddle steamer, the *Henry Venn*, just back from a long trip up the Niger past Onitsha and Lokoja and then even further up the River Benue.

"Yes, the *Henry Venn* had taken us farther than ever before," said Dandeson.

It was 1878. The *Henry Venn* was a gift from people in Britain who admired the work being done by the missionaries in West Africa. Money had been collected in Britain and the paddle boat had been built in the shipbuilding yards on the River Clyde in Scotland. The boat had provided much needed transport to visit the mission stations up river and had also enabled the missionaries to reach previously unexplored lands.

All the time there were threats of warfare in these regions. Ibadan was now a large and powerful town but had difficulty trading with Lagos. The Egba and the Ijebu people resented the power of Ibadan and made it impossible for people from that town to travel to and from the coast. Unfortunately in the battles that followed, people were often captured and used as slaves.

Onitsha was attacked and many buildings,

including the mission station, were burnt down. Bishop Crowther did all he could to maintain contact with his missions and even to build new ones. He was nearly seventy years of age but determined to continue his work. When the *Henry Venn* went on its long expedition up river to reach new territory up the River Benue, Bishop Crowther was disappointed that he was unable to go. His wife, Susan, was very ill and this time he did not feel able to leave her for such a long journey.

In spite of his age, Bishop Crowther always tried to set an example of hard work to those around him. On one occasion he arrived at Kipo Hill Mission station and found the mission building in a very poor state of repair. He asked about this and was told there was a shortage of building materials.

"Then we must make our own," said the bishop, who through the years had turned his hand to most practical things. Certainly he thought that brick making would not be beyond him. So he searched among the red and white sandstone clay hills around Kipo Hill and collected a quantity of clay for brick making. Then he practised making bricks, using a mould made for him by the village carpenter and finally baked the bricks on a fire. When he was satisfied with the bricks he had made, the bishop gathered all the workers at the mission around him and showed them what it was possible to make from the local clay.

"This clay comes from the hills nearby," he

explained. "There is more than enough of it to make us a mission house. Of course we will need hundreds of bricks but I'm going to show you how I have made these bricks you see before you."

The bishop then cut up the clay, moulded it into shape and baked it. The mission workers were very impressed by the results and praised their bishop for his skill but he laughed.

"It is mostly hard work and if we can all do this together we will soon have the mission house we need."

With such an example before them the others collected the clay and it was not long before Kipo Hill had its new building. This was typical of Bishop Crowther. He believed that hard work and determination could achieve most things and tried to show this by his own actions.

If the *Henry Venn* steamboat was away on a journey and the bishop needed to travel, he would not hesitate to go by canoe, alone if necessary but usually with Dandeson. These journeys were still dangerous, especially in the rainy season when the creeks and river estuary were lashed by violent storms.

Through the years Bishop Crowther had built up many friendships with chieftains of towns and villages in the Delta and along the Niger banks. They welcomed him and his Christian missions and helped him even in times of difficulty. There still were some chiefs however who were suspicious of the new missions. Sometimes they thought the missions wanted to interfere in village affairs. It was very difficult for Bishop Crowther to have any Christian influence in such a place.

On one occasion he heard that a chief living near to Benin wanted neither schools nor missions built in his village or even nearby. As usual when there were problems of this kind, it was the rainy season and travel overland was impossible.

"If I could reach this chief, I am sure I could persuade him that we come as friends to help his village," said Bishop Crowther.

"We have met this man before and he is not easy to persuade," said Dandeson. "If you wish to try, I will come with you, for travel even by canoe, will be hard."

Dandeson knew that his father had made his mind up to go and soon they were on their way in the canoe. The rain poured down for much of their journey and Dandeson was concerned for his father's health.

"It may not be possible to reach this chief," said Dandeson. "Perhaps it would be better if we turned back."

"If we turn back now, it would mean a long delay which is always a bad thing," said the bishop.

So they continued in spite of the storms and at last reached the village where the chieftain lived. They made their way ashore and were well received by the people of the village. The chieftain invited them to enjoy a meal of palm oil chop and took them through a courtyard to a small room, lit by oil lamps made from fragments of calabash which had been dipped in oil and arranged in a lid. This gave a flickering light, enough to see to eat and talk.

After they had finished the polite greetings and talk, Bishop Crowther mentioned the schools and mission stations he had built in other villages. He explained how both the children and adults had benefited and how Christianity taught people to be kind and friendly to each other. The chieftain's reply was to ask them to come with him at the end of the meal.

They followed him to another room where a young boy sat writing. It was the chieftain's son.

"You can see that he reads and writes well," said the chief. "There is no need for a school for the Sekeri people."

The bishop and Dandeson agreed that he could read and write already and praised the boy.

"There is so much for the Sekeri people to do and book learning alone is not good for them," the chief insisted.

"If you have a Christian mission it will not be just a place of book learning and neither will any school that we open for you," said Dandeson. "All true Christians are workers in every way."

"No, your mission would make my people lazy, just sitting about with books all day," said the chief.

"Yes and they would become rude and conceited to their elders," said the boy.

Again the bishop argued that the Bible taught people to be good, kind and respectful to their elders. Hour after hour they argued in a friendly way but neither side would give way. By the early hours of the morning when the calabash lamps had been relit many times, the argument still went on and at last the bishop could see he would never be able to persuade the chief of the Sekeri people to allow a school and a mission to be built in his village. Sadly and reluctantly but in a friendly manner, the bishop and his son said goodbye to the chief and left in their canoe.

They returned safely to their home, exhausted by a journey made in conditions of constant thunder storms and of heavy rain. Dandeson wondered just how much longer his father would be able to endure this kind of travelling to carry out his mission work. In fact, in spite of his age, Bishop Crowther continued to show amazing stamina to continue his Christian duties.

By 1877, the bishop and his wife Susan were able to celebrate their golden wedding anniversary. They had a happy family and a long life of achievement that they could look back on together. Susan's health was not good however and one day in 1880, when the bishop returned from a river journey on the *Henry Venn*, he found his wife very ill. Medical attention did not improve her health to any extent and her condition worsened. She died on 18 October that year and was buried at Christ Church, Lagos.

11

THE END OF A LIFE'S WORK

BISHOP Crowther was now over seventy. Although his wife had died he still had his family and many friends to sustain him in his life's work. He could be proud that there were Christian churches in towns all over the Niger territories which he had started years before and were now flourishing. He had done much for education in West Africa, being the first person to put the Yoruba language into writing and to produce books himself written in Yoruba. In 1852 he had been the first to write a Grammar and Vocabulary of Yoruba.

All these achievements had only come about after great effort and often after taking dangerous risks. With his Christian workers Crowther had worked on in spite of warfare and other problems. The mission stations had often been attacked and the missionaries killed and injured. By 1880, there were eleven mission stations that had survived and needed the attention of the bishop. In every case the missions were run by a staff of African missionaries.

In 1884 Bishop Crowther was on a steamboat called the *Qualaba*. As he had done for so many years, he was on a tour of visits to his missions, checking on progress and making notes of urgent needs. It was February and the dry season as the boat chugged its way up river past villages that were now so familiar to the bishop and Dandeson.

One evening he received a message that his aged mother had died and he wrote his feelings in his diary. "During my absence up the Niger my aged mother had been called to rest at the advanced age of ninety-seven years. After twenty-five years of separation through the violence of slave war, we were brought together again through God's good providence at Abeokuta in 1846. I told her then that she must not expect that I should be stationary at home with her as other members of the family would be, because I was a travelling public servant."

All through the years that Crowther had been a travelling public servant for Christianity, British merchants had been increasingly active trading along the banks of the Niger. By November 1879, Sir George Goldie had joined all the big traders into one company called the United African Company. This became the National African Company in 1882 and Sir George Goldie was given authority by the British Government to make trading agreements with African chieftains. By 1886, the Niger Company had been granted a royal charter and became the Royal Niger Company. For the next fourteen years this company controlled the main river trading areas and fixed the boundaries of Nigeria.

Bishop Crowther, still active in the organisation of his many mission stations, found that he and his missionaries were working alongside the officials of the Royal Niger Company. The boundaries created by the Company were often artificial and arranged for trading purposes. There were more than 250 tribal groups in Nigeria with their own religions, languages and culture. Some of the groups found that land that had once been theirs was now given to some other tribe. This caused bad feeling and conflict.

In 1882 Bishop Crowther went for the last time on a visit to England. He discussed with British leaders the problems facing the Christian missions. Some of these difficulties still involved the need for more money and missionaries for West Africa. Then there were the new problems created by the policies of the Royal Niger Company.

As usual the bishop was well received and listened to with respect as an expert on Christian affairs in West Africa. He was seventy-three years of age and his work was still demanding. Perhaps the time had come for him to step aside and let some younger man take over. The committee in London did not want to hear such talk. The bishop still looked amazingly fit and well and in any case his experience and knowledge of Yoruba made him indispensable. They told him they would like him to go on with his Christian work for as long as he wished.

Apart from his usual duties as a bishop and his contribution to the Yoruba language, he had other achievements of which he could be proud. His travels as a missionary over many years had taken him to remote areas of West Africa never before seen. Wherever he went he made notes and kept a diary. So there was always a record of what he had done and the things he had seen. Much of his studies in geography were of great value to people outside Africa such as universities and companies wishing to know about the possibilities for trade.

His research work on geographical conditions in various regions of West Africa were recognised in Britain. As a result he was granted the Diploma of Fellow of the Royal Geographical Society. His dictionary in Yoruba, brought up to date, continued to be a reference book into the twentieth century. In the same way, his translations of parts of the Bible, prayer and hymn books into Yoruba continued to be used in Nigerian Christian churches.

He continued in his work until severe illness struck him down during September 1891. He suffered a stroke which caused loss of movement in his right arm and leg. In addition his speech was affected, but his determination was as strong as ever. He still hoped and believed that he would get better and go to his missions yet again to help.

The bishop had been advised to rest away from his work and to do this he was sent by his doctor to Bonny. Here he began to feel a little better and wrote to a friend that if he continued to improve he would soon be able to resume his normal work. His hand trembled as he wrote however, showing that his health was still poor.

He went back to Lagos to be looked after by his

daughter Abigail Macaulay. Her husband was the Principal of Lagos Grammar School and she took a great interest in education. She discussed school affairs with her father, read letters and extracts of books to him and generally looked after him. The bishop's grandson, Charles, was also good company for his grandfather, chatting and reading to him and making him feel cheerful.

Bishop Crowther still kept his diary up to date. On Christmas Day, 1891, he insisted on going to the morning church service. Although he was getting weaker he still wanted to attend church services. It was planned that he should return to Bonny in the New Year.

As his right leg and hand were paralysed, he had difficulty in moving about the house. Yet he thought constantly about his mission stations far away and wondered if all was well with the Christian workers who were still struggling against great difficulties. Some were in rain forests near the coast, their missions reached through a network of creeks and lagoons. How he would have loved to have gone on another trip up river in one of the latest steamers.

All the time, in spite of his illness, he hoped that somehow this might be possible. The sad truth was that he felt very tired and was getting weaker although he would not admit it.

"Can I do something that will take me outside the house?" He asked his doctor one day.

"At this moment it is best that you should rest and do nothing," said the doctor.

Bishop Crowther complained about this and continued to insist that he would soon be well again. On 31 December he wrote in his diary, grumbling that he was not allowed to do anything. "But," he added, "I am getting better."

Friends still called to see him and one that evening was an elderly lady named Emma Taiwo. She had heard that he might soon be going to Bonny and wanted to wish him well.

"If he is tired, I won't talk to him for long," Emma promised as Abigail greeted her.

As soon as Emma saw the bishop however, she noticed he was slumped to one side of the sofa and she called Abigail at once. Abigail made him comfortable and when he shivered she fetched brandy and water which seemed to revive him. Then they sent for the doctor.

When Doctor Baudle came, he said that the Bishop must stay in bed. With Abigail one side of him and the doctor the other, Bishop Crowther was able to stand and then walk slowly to his bedroom.

"I want him to take this medicine," said the doctor. "Tomorrow I will call again to see how he is."

Abigail did as Doctor Baudle had asked and kept a careful watch on her father that evening. When she asked him how he felt, he smiled and tried to reassure her that he was suffering no pain.

There was no more that either Abigail or the doctor could do. Bishop Crowther's life and work were over. He died after midnight on New Year's Eve and was buried on 1 January, next to his wife in Christchurch Cathedral in Lagos.

Bishop Crowther's work for his Christian beliefs was his permanent memorial but his friends in Britain and Africa made sure that his name would not be forgotten. There is a large east window dedicated to his memory in Christchurch Cathedral and churches in Nigeria and Sierra Leone are named after him. Nearly eight years after he died, a marble monument was erected in Lagos in his honour. These were suitable tributes to the ex-slave boy who had spread the Christian message to so many parts of West Africa.